MW01636014

Ten New Hotels
Europe 2006

Edited by Laurent Vernhes

Ten New Hotels
Europe 2006

Tablet Hotels

Contents

Introduction

Tablet Hotels is the cure for boring travel – the one-stop prescription shop for the jaded and harried traveler. We can't tell you who you should be traveling with, and frankly, it's none of our business. In the area of choosing a hotel and getting the best price for it, however, we feel we have some expertise to offer. We aim to provide the kind of tips one would expect from a friend.

If, like us, you are obsessed with hotels, then you will agree that we are living in happy times. A wide variety of talents and a considerable amount of money are converging on the hospitality industry. More and more hoteliers are focusing on providing travelers with unique experiences, rather than just a checklist of services and amenities.

A few years ago, a new independent hotel opening was news in itself. These days, the question is which one of the myriad of new hotels we read about in each month's crop of magazines is destined to become a classic. Even some of the large corporate chains have come up with truly inspired offerings.

This book is the first in a series presenting our selection of the best newly built or renovated hotels. Before selecting them, we give them a few months to work through the challenges inevitably associated with starting something new. Then we look beyond the PR noise, stay there anonymously, and see what's come together. We are continually inspired and fascinated by anyone who has the initiative and discipline to make their visions real. This series of books will be our tribute to those creators (hoteliers and designers) who have taken that step and achieved excellence in the past twelve months.

For the purposes of this series, we have divided the world into four regions: Europe, the Americas, Asia, and Africa/Oceania. Every year we'll select ten new hotels from each region, and publish the results. Stay tuned – amazing new hotels are opening all the time!

Laurent Vernhes
Co-founder and CEO

L'Andana
Grosseto, Italy

L'Andana occupies a particularly auspicious parcel of land near western Tuscany's Tyrrhenian coast – Tenuta La Badiola was once the hunting estate of the Grand Duke Leopold II, and today is as picturesque a collection of vineyards and sun-drenched foothills as one is likely to find anywhere in Italy. Despite this well-bred heritage, the estate's aristocratic connection is traded on rather lightly, trumped by an association with a more current name, that of one of its co-owners, the French star chef Alain Ducasse.

A seasoned hotel chef and auberge operator, Ducasse once vowed to stay out of Italy, only to be tempted by the sheer magic of this location, a few miles inland from the seaside town of Castiglione della Pescaia. Here you're remote enough to hide out for a while, if that's your style, yet equally well placed to see the sights, near enough to places like Siena and Lucca and the scenic Maremma coast to make for easy day-tripping.

It's not only about convenience, of course: this is the storybook Tuscan landscape, where the sun hangs low over the foothills, casting its golden light over rows of grapevines and olive trees. And it's apparent upon arrival that

you're on to something special – the half-mile driveway, lined with cypresses and umbrella pines, makes for a stunning first impression.

The hotel itself amply delivers on this promise, with its rooms and suites spread across the duke's old villa and the connected farmhouse. Interiors are by the Italian editor of Architectural Digest, Ettore Mochetti, and are sophisticated, eschewing faux-rustic country clichés in favor of a more urbane and opulent look. After all, the mock unpretentiousness of the first-class country inn is no less a carefully considered pose than any other, and there's something refreshingly honest these days about a rural luxury hotel that dares to look luxurious.

Gone, then, are the crumbling, unpainted surfaces and the slightly mismatched antique furnishings you might expect to see in a more typical farmhouse hotel. These pieces, though designed in an antique style, are custom-built and as new as the morning paper, set against a backdrop of sponge-painted pastel walls and shining new hardwood floors. Sofas are impossibly decadent and even the chaise in the bathroom (that's right) is comfortable enough to sleep on, should the urge to nap take you by surprise on your way to or from the oversized bath.

As for the atmosphere, it's a slightly odd blend of professional hospitality and guest-house intimacy, with breakfast ordered in the kitchen, right over the cook's shoulder, and served in the drawing rooms or out on the patio. For dinner it's over to the restaurant, a hundred-yard walk across the grounds to the old granary building, where a simple Tuscan cuisine is delivered with flourishes of Ducassian wit, accompanied by wines from L'Andana co-owner Vittorio Moretti's vineyards. Ingredients are fresh and unmediated, as is the current vogue, many, like the olive oil, produced on the grounds.

The old estate boasts some thousand-plus acres to explore at your leisure, and closer to home is the pool, where it's not uncommon to find your fellow guests passing entire afternoons soaking in the sunshine. There's an outdoor squash court that looks a bit underused and a new nine-hole golf course. Despite the estate's hunting-lodge heritage, the sporting life, it seems, is less popular an attraction than the epicurean charms and quiet restfulness of the place. And if, as is likely, you'd like to take a bit of the dining experience home with you, the hotel's kitchen offers courses in Italian cooking, training would-be Ducasses on the finer points of Tuscany's culinary traditions.

NON
DISTURBARE

Aceto
Balsamico
di Modena

STAURANT
Zetter
Open all day
Lunch &

The Zetter Restaurant & Rooms
London, England

London is a notoriously expensive hotel market, a city where visitors are forced to choose between fabulously stylish hotels at stratospheric prices and barely habitable ones at rates that are merely high.

It's a welcome change, then, to find a new London hotel that manages to be impressive yet comparatively inexpensive. The Zetter Restaurant & Rooms sidesteps the high-luxury arms race, focusing instead on an under-served audience: not the power-shoppers and museum-goers of the West End hotels, but rather the sort of people you're likely to spy from the Zetter restaurant window as they walk down Clerkenwell Road – architects, graphic designers, Hoxton artists and dealers, perhaps even the occasional young City banker in a pinstripe suit.

This crowd, well accustomed to loft conversions and other reclaimed spaces, has taken to the Zetter's cheeky blend of retro and futuristic. Flat grey surfaces and white down duvets set the backdrop, and some modern hotel decorators would stop there – here splashes of bright color and the

occasional beanbag or Louis XV chair keep things from getting sterile. A bedside lamp cycles through the color spectrum, equal parts mood ring and high-tech lava lamp, and at the flick of a red switch, the room is bathed in a deep pink light, a bit much for kicking back in bed with one of the Penguin classics from the bookshelf, but possibly quite suited for entertaining. It's design-conscious, to be sure, but with a human touch, more playground than museum perhaps, an environment that responds to the touch as well as the look.

Equally noteworthy, though perhaps less immediately apparent to the casual observer, is the sustainable approach taken to the building's conversion. A reclaimed industrial district known for its derelict printing presses and its run-down warehouses is not perhaps the first place you'd look for eco-friendly architecture; nevertheless, the Zetter carries some impressive green credentials.

Architects Chetwood Associates, best known for their sustainable Sainsbury's supermarket at Greenwich Peninsula, have worked their environmentally conscious magic on this site as well, using cold water from the near-forgotten London Aquifer to absorb waste heat, saving space and electricity by eliminating the need for a massive central air-conditioning apparatus, and to flush waste water, reducing the demand on London's clean drinking water. Access to pressurized water at a constant temperature also means less space need be given over to water storage, thus increasing the number of guest rooms, a bottom-line benefit you don't have to be a Greenpeace member to appreciate.

The restaurant benefits from the water-drilling scheme as well: filtered, bottled water from the aquifer beneath the hotel is available on every table, not just as a tangible assertion of the Zetter's personality, but as a subtle reminder of the hotel's environmentally sound approach. First-time hotel owners Mark Sainsbury and Michael Benyan have quite a bit of previous restaurant experience, and the Zetter's Italian restaurant has become a neighborhood favorite on its own – no mean feat for a hotel dining room. Lunch and dinner guests breeze past the slight and unimposing hotel reception, past the lounge and up a few steps to the restaurant, where sunlight pours in through full-length windows.

Making the most of the available light was another of Chetwood's inspirations; perhaps a counterintuitive move in grey London, but one that has paid off in spades. A central atrium runs the height of the building, allowing sunlight to stream through openings in the roof panels and illuminate the corridors of all five residential floors, down to the lobby lounge. Top-floor penthouses were

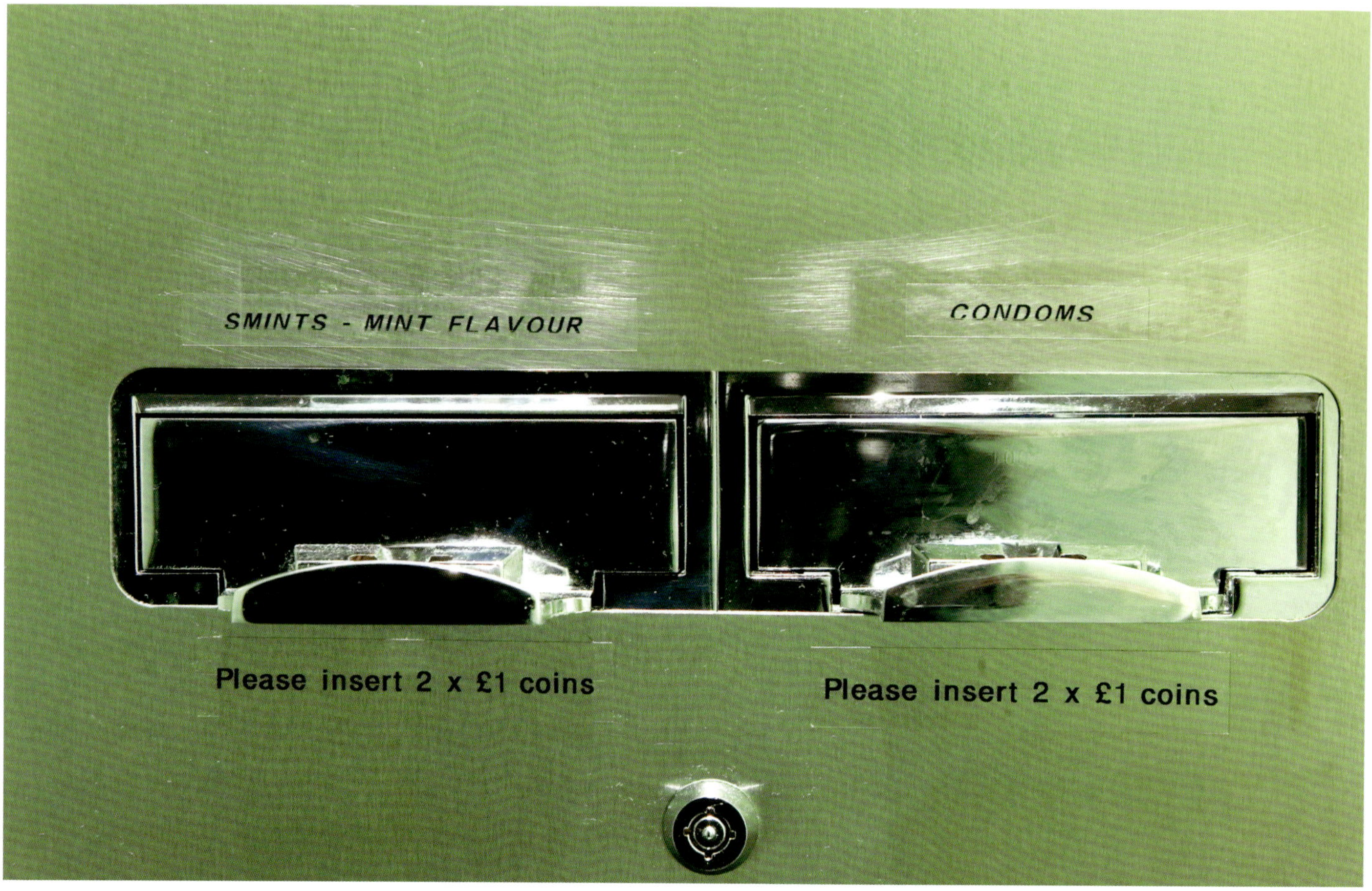

added, below the lines of sight of the surrounding streets, in conformity with local regulations – rooms are set back from the building's edge, resulting in a handful of private decks, sunny miniature gardens with views of the rooftops of Clerkenwell and the City.

The Zetter's guests care about inventive solutions to these kinds of problems, in a way the people who stay at the Ritz or the Savoy may not. The young creative professionals who stay here for the inspiring design and the lively atmosphere are only all too happy to go along with the hotel's energy-saving measures, and the fairly modest rates only add to the appeal. Booking a stylish and intelligent hotel around Clerkenwell for under two hundred pounds is just the smart thing to do.

INTERVIEW WITH MARK SAINSBURY, OWNER OF THE ZETTER RESTAURANT & ROOMS

What was the concept for the Zetter?
We were thinking there's got to be a way that we could offer quirkiness and design edge, but without the price tag. In fact, the original idea was that we would aim for a hundred pounds a night, no room service, no porters, and we started looking for a property on that basis – and realized that if we wanted a property we could afford, it would be out in the sticks, halfway to Heathrow. In central London you've got to charge a bit more and therefore you've got to offer a bit more.

Was it a difficult birth process?
Yeah, a very difficult pregnancy, definitely. The problem being that my partner Michael and I had never done this before. We'd opened a restaurant up the road called Moro, but this made Moro feel like a breeze in comparison. Every decision we made was that much more tortured, and we didn't have anything to judge it against – our judgement was based on instinct rather than experience, and that made it tricky.

That said, all our designers were lovely to work with, and in a way were more accommodating than they should have been. Our architects were very client-driven, and never told us to stop meddling or interfering or suggesting. It was very friendly, we all got on really well, but actually we could have done with a bit more discipline. I think it's a pretty unusual thing for an architect to tell a client what I'm asking, you know, to shut up, but we could have done with that.

What drew you to Chetwood Associates?
Chetwood's came in and just blew us away. They talked the right language: engineering value added, the borehole water cooling, the environmental credentials, recycled materials, energy-efficient systems, and so on. What they offered to us was this quite rare combination of the commercial and the innovative. They had the size and experience to think of the commercial reality of this hotel, and the kind of flair or design edge that we were looking for.

Your vision changed as a result of the realities of London real estate, but was it further altered by the collaboration with Chetwood's?
The overall concept, not so much, I have to say. They certainly squeezed more rooms out of the building than ever we thought we could. We came to the table with a pretty developed idea of what we wanted. The environmental aspect was always important to us, but we didn't know what it really meant to be a green hotel, nor what options we had. They helped us with that.

Are you already thinking about the next hotel?
Yeah, I think we are. What shape that would take is

absolutely up for discussion. One of the main things we were reacting against was this chain hotel status quo. For the building to reflect its immediate environment and respect its own fabric is incredibly important. In other words, I'd hate to do a Zetter 2.

In London, real estate is such a big deal. We took two years to find this building. We're just going to start looking at buildings, in the areas of London we think are exciting, and match the idea to the building rather than the other way round. So we'll see. There are lots of different ideas – we'll wait till we find the property first.

What lessons have you learned here that you'll take away to the next one?
Don't procure it like we did – structure the whole thing differently. Do your design up front – don't design on the go. More discipline on cost control.
We made a lot of mistakes in the restaurant. We'd done one before, and hadn't done a hotel, so we gave the hotel all our time, and imagined the restaurant would look after itself. So we were naive on that front, and I won't make that same mistake. Just because you've done something before doesn't mean that you know it all.

What's your favorite hotel?
There's a wonderful one outside of Florence in Fiesole called Villa San Michele. I do have time for Schrager, I have to say; I think he's done some amazing things. I like St. Martins Lane. My cousin Jessica Sainsbury has got a place just outside Cheltenham called Cowley Manor – fantastic. And we had a great time staying in the Post Ranch Inn in Big Sur.

I like the Firmdale hotels. We talk about them a lot actually. They did their first one, and they took a long time to do the second, and they got it right. Now they're opening one a year, at least, and doing it very quickly. Tim's wife, Kit, the interior designer, she's got a really fantastic feel.

INTERVIEW WITH LAURIE CHETWOOD, ARCHITECT OF THE ZETTER RESTAURANT & ROOMS

How did you become involved in this project?
We won the project on an environmental approach, and getting more rooms into the building. The environmental side was to use the London Aquifer. It comes up at 12 degrees, so it's cool, and it's constant, more or less, so you can use it to dump excess heat. It also reduces water storage – rooms were obviously at a premium so any space taken up by water storage was a pain in the neck.

We brought the water up and we proposed to use it in three different ways. One was to cool the kitchens and the rooms, two was to flush the loos, and three was to bottle it, to put it on the restaurant table, so you actually get filtered, bottled water. But actually the more practical use is it didn't take up much space.

What was Mark's original vision for this hotel?
We were aiming at young professionals staying in London. They wanted the design to be cool and sophisticated, but not too cool, not too sophisticated, and on the other hand they didn't want it to be too gimmicky either. I think you can see it's a pleasant blend, due to the fact that they had strong views as to how they should furnish it.

What was the balance between interpreting the owners' vision and expressing your own?
It was their first hotel, so the process was new to them, but they had pretty strong ideas. It was a joint effort. You can see the architectural bit, and then you can see the layer of the stylist on top, and then you can see the other layer, Mark and his business partner, Mike. You can see those three layers running through it and I think it's quite a nice way of doing it.

Are there any other hotels that you find particularly inspiring?
I do like the Sanderson, I must say. It's got surprises all over it. It definitely wasn't the hotel that Mark was looking for, that style, but it's got Starck all over it, with daft things here and there and everywhere, and even going to the lift is fun.

How would this differ from a hotel you financed yourself?
Personally, I'd have more surprises in it. I do like surprise in a hotel. It's probably not the most commercially safe thing to do. My wife and I have just done a house which is completely mad, and I like that idea.

It depends on the hotel but I would really rev up the emotional side of it. Take a few chances, I suppose, be creative about how you approach the design concept, not just the design.

Are you and Mark planning more hotels?
I'm not sure if they are. If you thought about it, the way that they approached this hotel, they might do something completely different somewhere else. They're very eclectic, as I said, and if they were looking for something completely different I can imagine they might look for a completely different architect. Obviously we'd like to work with them again, but I can see them perhaps getting a fresh approach for a fresh hotel somewhere else. But I don't know whether they're thinking of that or not.

Were there any lessons learned on this one that you think might apply to the next?
I think so. You must establish the brief as well as you can, and boil the brief down to the essence of the building. Then when all the decisions keep coming up, you check back to the essence of the building and say, is this actually what you wanted?

Architects are useless at taking a brief. You get a picture in your head and you start designing. I think we should spend more time fixing the essence of the building, and we've now got in place a proper process which brings in lots of different people to get the brief right. The advertising industry have things called account planners – a person who sits between the creative people and the client, checking that the brief is consistently adhered to. We have installed an account planner, if you like, for us.

Would you rather build a church or a stadium?
A church. I've always wanted to do that. I think if you ask anybody, what was the last time you went into a building and got a sort of tingle, an emotional thing, most people would say a cathedral or a church.

The thing I like about cathedrals is that apart from probably taste, it hits all the senses. But it should really be the same for most buildings. You should be able to get that tingle factor in different ways in all buildings. The technology is there to do much more, but architects play it pretty safe at the moment. It's all ninety degrees, minimal, and people want more than that, I think.

The Bvlgari Hotel
Milano, Italy

You'd never know you were in Milan. Certainly the cutting edge interiors, the high-design furnishings and fittings, the sleek efficiency of the place all speak to a decidedly Milanese influence. But looking over the edge of the balcony, onto a manicured garden, like something from a Zen monastery, surrounded by tall trees – if you didn't know better, you'd never believe you were in a city hotel, much less one located at the heart of Italy's economic engine, a grey and smoggy city abuzz with activity, its harried residents hard at work, too busy making money to set aside time for a stroll down a garden path.

The phenomenal location is key to the Bulgari's pervasive calm, with almost pastoral surroundings courtesy of a prime situation in the upscale Brera district, at the end of a private street, with the Botanical Gardens for a neighbor. The building itself, though, is no less tranquil; arriving up the cobbled drive, you're greeted by soft-spoken staffers in unstructured grey suits. Once off the lift, the thick carpeting in the dimly lit corridors absorbs all sound of footfall, and the rooms are so well soundproofed you'd be forgiven for feeling that you were the hotel's only guest.

Inside, a flat-screen television plays a sort of abstract light show, accompanied by calming music, while the room's high-tech lighting system projects a serene glow from nowhere in particular. Creams and blacks predominate, the bathroom floors and walls hewn from black Zimbabwe granite, the showers and surfaces from travertine, the doors and fixtures in the bedroom made from oak and teak. A deep tub hides behind a screen of woven metal threads.

There's a desk with a built-in internet connection and an office chair, but it's difficult to think of work when so much of the voluminous space is given over to the towering bed, with its assortment of pillows in multiple sizes, and the bath, nearly large enough to be a private salon. Given the high proportion of fashion-industry guests the Bulgari receives, especially during fashion week, the expansive closets could count in the office column; for the rest of us, though, they're a luxury, outfitted with accessories like a shoe horn for babying your Ferragamos and a full-size umbrella for braving the Northern weather.

For all the Bulgari's design bona fides – and the design holds its own against the most stylish boutique you can name – the experience is one of luxury, full stop. The L-word is not one that carries much currency with us at present, as the prevailing conception of luxury involves a lot of white gloves, caviar and gilt, with showmanship taking the place of practical comforts, pomp replacing design. Too many of the world's top luxury hotels live in a world of carefully preserved yet historically indeterminate nostalgia, attempting to impress the modern guest with a packaged version of a glamorous age gone by.

To step into the Bulgari, one imagines, is to feel much as one would have felt walking into Europe's grand hotels in their Twenties or 1890s heyday, when Art Nouveau was the cutting edge of architecture and interior design, when the simplicity of Art Deco was positively revolutionary. The Bulgari is luxurious, by any reasonable definition of the word, yet it's completely of its moment, representing the finest materials, craftsmanship and design available today.

Of course in creating an environment like this, it helps to have a master's hand. The Bulgari's designer was the hometown hero Antonio Citterio, one of Milan's leading architects and one of the world's legends of industrial design. The fixtures and fittings are not just stylish and upmarket, with taps and basins by Axor and lamps by Flos, but they're the next best thing to custom-designed – they're a selection of Citterio's best industrial design work, a sort of greatest hits collection that fits seamlessly into his interiors.

The result is a textbook example of what great design can do for a hotel. Not just fashionable eye candy, Citterio's design runs deep, orchestrating large spaces and small details into a unified and uniquely sedate experience for the visitor. Top-quality plumbing and electronics means everything works smoothly and effortlessly, with a dizzying selection of lighting permutations easily controllable from a small remote. And the sheer solidity of the materials – whether the custom-cut granite slabs of the bathrooms or even just the impossible thickness of the sheets and towels – intensifies the tactile experience, achieving a sense of richness and luxury that most hotels can't match.

For all the monastic calm of the sequestered and soundproofed guest rooms, the Bulgari's public spaces draw something of a crowd, especially in the evening. The hotel's restaurant is popular for lunch and dinner, serving simple yet fine Mediterranean cuisine. The bar does a rollicking business at night, attracting wealthy Milanese and hotel guests alike, as the excitement spills out from the restaurant terrace to the gardens, set with lounge chairs and lanterns.

In the basement, a surprise: the underground spa, a place that feels like one of Milan's most delightful secrets. Treatment rooms and fitness rooms branch off the corridors, but the pool is the centerpiece, inlaid with tile, glittering gold and green. Above one end in a translucent green glass cube is the steam room, and outside a small alcove with sofa seating open to the sky.

Though the concept may meet with some skepticism, the Bulgari is as close as any earthly hotel to the Platonic ideal of the urban resort. Inside the walls it's all calm serenity, surrounded by leafy gardens and seemingly miles from urban Milan; but a few steps past the front gate in either direction are the Scala opera house and the Golden Rectangle of designer shops along Via Montenapoleone. All the charms of the metropolis at your fingertips, and yet none of the sounds and stresses of city life – it sounds simple but the Bulgari is one of just a few places to meet the description, making it a special hotel indeed.

94% of all hotel guests expect no surprises when entering their room.

Hotel Fox
Copenhagen, Denmark

Corporate-owned and committee-designed chain hotels are the reason for Tablet Hotels' existence; or, more properly, they are the force we struggle against every day. It may be beyond irony, then, to chronicle the genesis of Copenhagen's Hotel Fox, a hotel whose conception and design are the complete antithesis of the chain hotel norm, and a place where even the conventions and familiar tropes of the independent "boutique" hotel are challenged and subverted over and over again.

It's no coincidence that the hotel bears the name of a popular German car: Project Fox was commissioned by Volkswagen as a part of the 2005 launch of the newest incarnation of its compact Fox automobile, and was intended as ground zero for a dizzying press offensive. Hundreds of journalists would pass through the hotel during the three weeks of the launch event, and no effort was spared in convincing them of the vibrant and youthful energy of the new Fox.

At this point some skepticism might be warranted, especially in the current corporate-shy intellectual climate. But Italian art would have been all the poorer without the Medicis; likewise today's advertising-driven variety of corporate

patronage is a lifeline to the artistic communities, jump-starting countless careers and exposing artist after artist to a public they might not have been able to reach through do-it-yourself channels.

And to post-launch hotel guests, what matters is the result. The Hotel Fox is stunning, an overwhelming and eye-popping graphic experience, one that shames even the most adventurous boutique hotels, and one that's hardly recognizable as being of the same species as the typical chain hotel stay. Would it be somehow more pure an experience if your hundred-odd euros per night went to line the coffers of a local property developer or an ambitious restaurant impresario?

In any case, you'll quickly forget about the hotel's sponsorship once you're safely in the hands of the twenty-one artists, graphic designers and illustrators selected to execute the Fox's astonishing makeover. The overriding feeling is one of relentless positivity, a colorful and kinetic experience that's a welcome contrast with the sedate and moody atmosphere of the boutique-hotel standard, and the artists draw heavily on graffiti and street art, the polar opposites of the minimalism and high modernism that inspire too many contemporary interiors.

A description of the Fox's more remarkable elements would read like a list of objects you never thought you'd see in a hotel: gangs of stuffed animals, vinyl tape as a structural element, even a well-used punching bag hanging from the ceiling of one boxing-themed room. Each room is not just different but wildly different from all the others, and each bears a conceptual element that's a bit more thought-provoking than the blank-slate approach of the traditional hotel space. Some rooms are overtly sexual in theme and decoration, a departure from the implicit but never stated sex appeal of the modern boutique, while others refer to childhoods real or imagined, surrealistic dream states, or language and typography.

Two elements were held constant amid all the frenzied experimentation: beds are standard, at least beneath the highly individual bed coverings, and the bathrooms are consistent as well, though hardly boring, featuring playful Philippe Starck toilets and brightly colored rubber shower heads by Agape. It would be far-fetched to claim that the Fox experience is all about such basics as comfy beds and functional bathrooms, but it's reassuring to know you're not in for any unsavory surprises in these departments.

All the visual excess of the Hotel Fox makes it quite clear it's aimed at a younger demographic; reinforcing this impression is the fact that the room rates, for the time being, start around a hundred euros. This is a reasonable enough price anywhere in Europe, but in pricey Copenhagen it's positively a steal. Expect to rub elbows with design-conscious hipsters on a budget in the Milk & Honey bar, and if you find yourself with a strange craving for a new Volkswagen, at least you'll know where it came from.

8 PERSONER
ELLER
600 KG GODS
4
3
4
1
2
LOBBY
-1
-2
PANDA$

FOX

A NICE DAY.

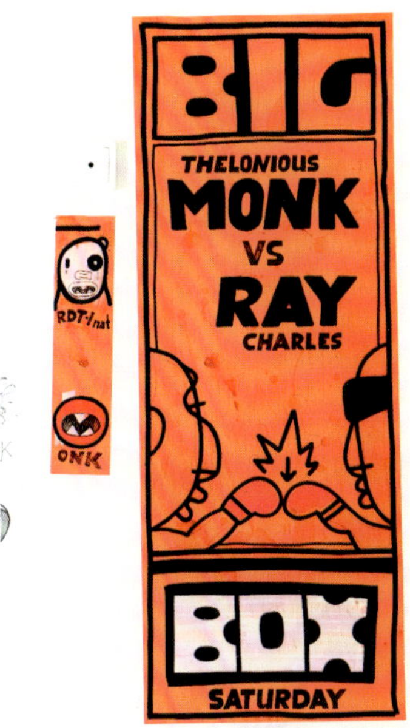

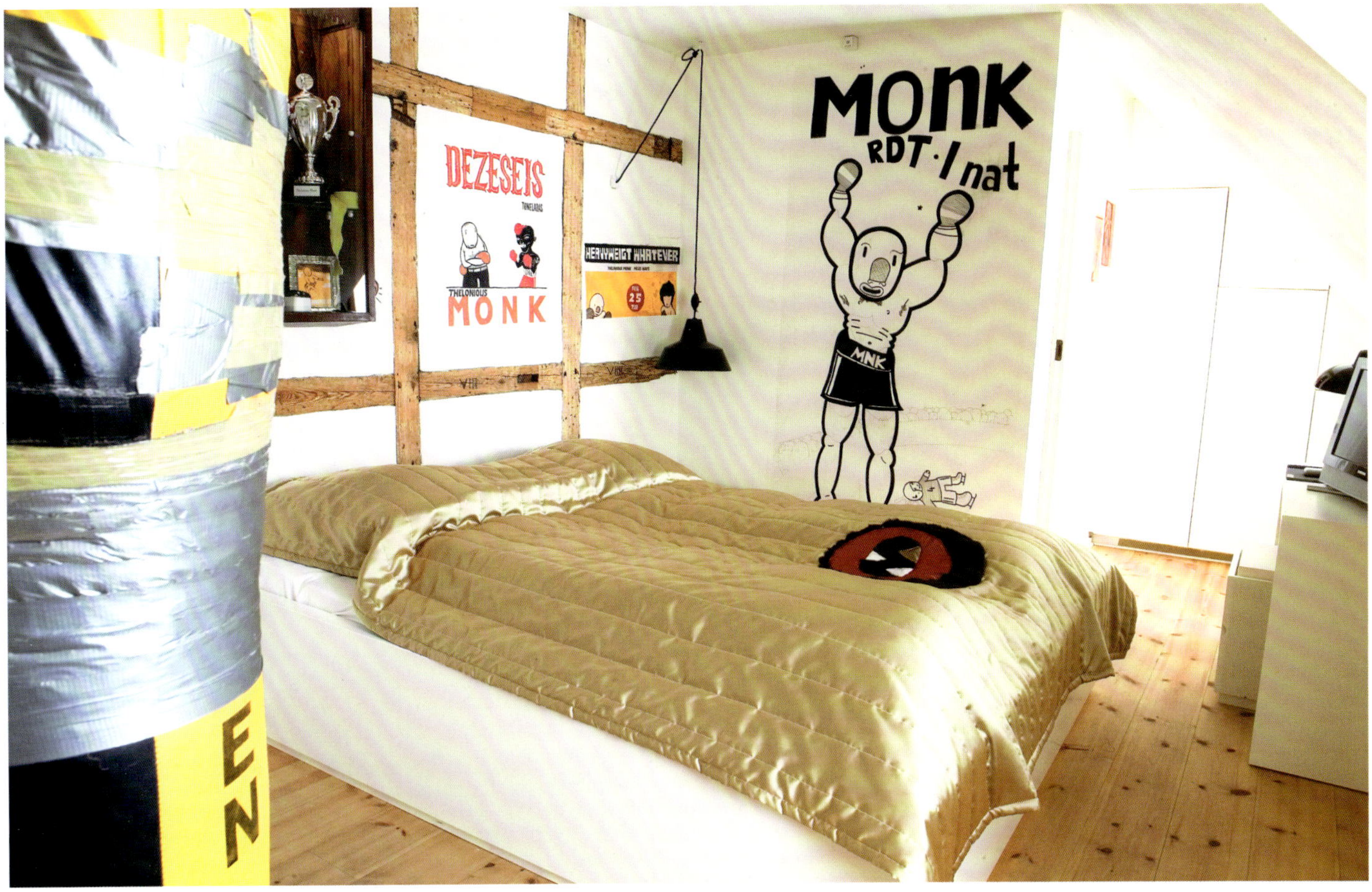
DEZESEIS
THELONIOUS
MONK
HEAVYWEIGT WHATEVER
MONK
RDT·I nat
MNK

RDT·I nat
ONK
BIG
THELONIOUS
MONK
VS
RAY
CHARLES
BOX
SATURDAY

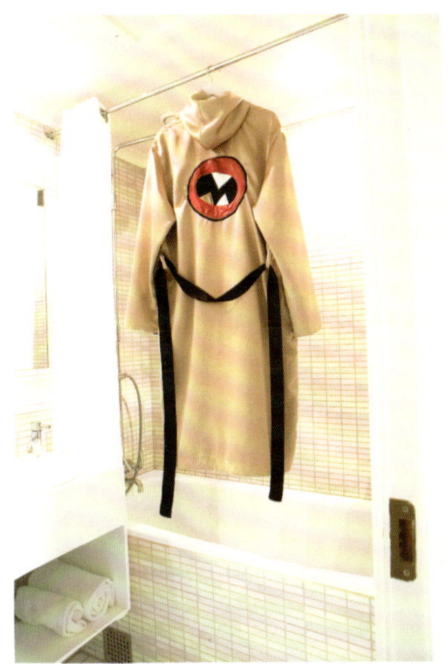

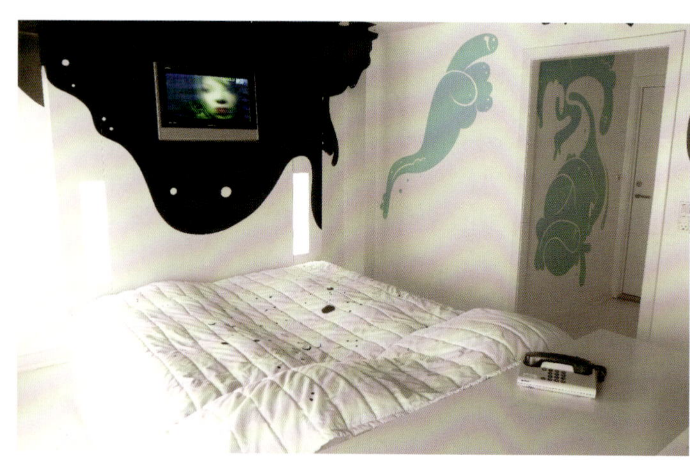

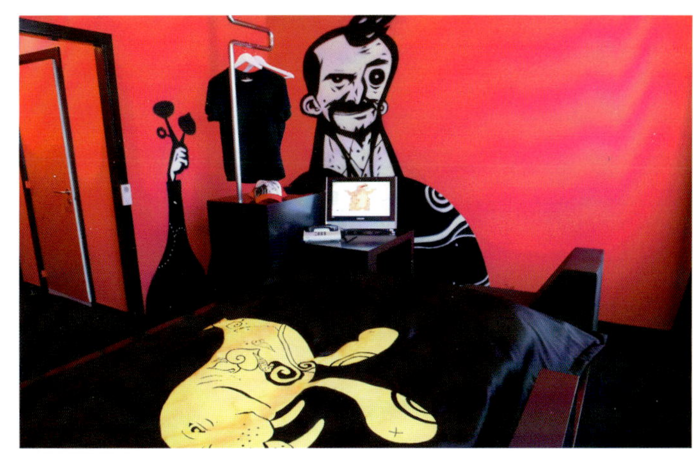

108

The....
CROWN

The
Royal
WEDDING

WELCOME

THE SECRET PALACE

The College Hotel
Amsterdam, Netherlands

The mind reels imagining the kind of grim and faceless establishments where today's hospitality graduates must have had their student work experience – airport hotels, perhaps, or neglected motor inns off little-used roadways.

In the Netherlands, at least, this is happily not the case. Students of the Roc, Amsterdam's top hospitality school, cut their teeth in a splendid 1894 brickwork building, once a college of economics, convincingly converted into a first-class modern hotel. Managed by the Stein Group of luxury hotels, and sister to the Dylan, among others, the College Hotel is anything but a student model – graduates, in fact, are likely to take a step down once they've entered the job market.

In a hotel staffed entirely by young students, service could understandably be a concern, no matter how experienced and firm-handed the management team. Good news here: while you won't run across the kind of seasoned professionals one encounters at other of the world's best hotels, neither will you be left to fend for yourself. There's nothing that can't be fixed in time, as the Stein Group's management team is never far from the scene.

One doesn't come to the Netherlands for obsequious service, and you'll likely find yourself charmed by the freshness and enthusiasm of the College's student

staff. There's no hint of pretentiousness to the place, despite the utterly current modern interiors, decorated in rather serious warm and muted tones – the look is more London-style boudoir luxury than spare Nordic minimalism. In fact, this is one of only two Dutch hotels we know to successfully venture into luxury and glamour – two words rarely associated with the best of Dutch design.

The guest rooms are immersive, dead quiet and as comfortable as can be, with ample space and all the modern conveniences. Not all of the bathrooms come with tubs, due to the vagaries of the building's original floor plan, but all are handsome, with glass-walled showers and tile and slate rather than marble.

The college's restaurant, housed in the old gymnasium, is unsurprisingly a wide-open space, split in half with the diners on the one side and the chefs on the other, only half hidden behind a mirrored partition – perhaps to reassure nervous diners that there is indeed something going on in that trainee kitchen. The cuisine is modern Dutch, slightly on the adventurous side, and the dining room does business as a proper restaurant, exposing the locals as well as the guests to the student-exam fare, to remarkably strong results. Also of note is the luxurious bar area, a warm and stylish place full of interior-design surprises, furnishing the added thrill of sipping cocktails poured by teenagers; file under "only in Amsterdam," perhaps.

It's a stunning contemporary hotel environment, designed to expose the students to the most discerning and demanding guests. Further enticement comes in the form of relatively modest rates, so even the occasional mistake should be easily forgiven. Nevertheless, with 140 staff members dedicated to servicing just 40 rooms, it's unlikely you'll feel left out to dry, and the youthful energy is positively contagious.

DO NOT
DISTURB

INTERVIEW WITH ROC VAN AMSTERDAM, OWNER OF THE COLLEGE HOTEL

What was your original vision for this hotel?
To build a hotel where students can practice hospitality at the highest level, where service is the most important part of the experience. Not only during the week, but weekends and holidays as well, 365 days out of the year. So the students can taste the world of real live international hospitality.

Was it a difficult or an easy birth process?
It was a very difficult process. It took almost seven years to realize the whole project, from the first meeting until the first guest arrived. During this process we had to deal with the government, the local hotels, the town council, the teachers, the students, the parents of the students... All of them had their own ideas about the hotel. It was important to find a balance between their visions and the original concept of the hotel.

How did you choose the architects?
We were looking for young professionals in the beginning of their careers, just like the hotel's students. An architect who can create a concept of a hotel, where there is an optimal balance between learning and working. Now we can say it was a very good choice. It was a little risky to choose these architects, because of their lack of experience – before the College Hotel they had created only some concepts for restaurants.

Are you already thinking about the next hotel?
I'm always thinking about new learning concepts. Last February I visited South Africa – maybe there is an opportunity in Cape Town or Pretoria. At this moment we are building a wellness center in the heart of Amsterdam, near the Carré. We hope it will be open in March. It's based on the same concept as the College Hotel: for students, run by students, for guests.

Describe the audience your hotel has found. Are they the sort of travelers you expected?
We have mostly business travelers during the week, and leisure guests during the weekends. Most of the guests come from the US, UK, France, Germany and Spain. The bar and restaurant are at the moment quite popular with the people of Amsterdam.

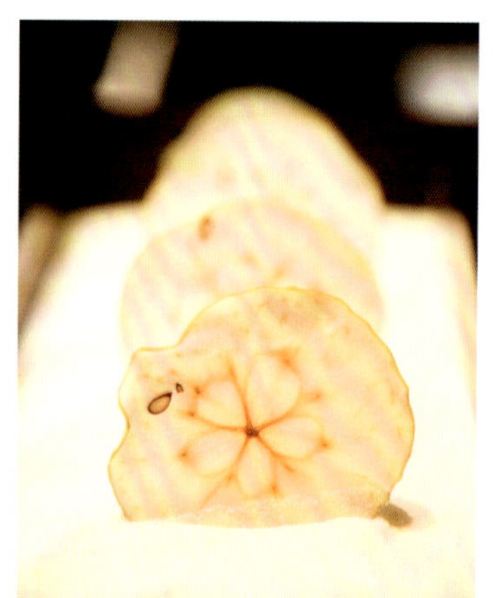

INTERVIEW WITH FG-STIJL, ARCHITECT OF THE COLLEGE HOTEL

What was the client's original vision for this hotel?
To create an institution where top students of the ROC can have practical experience in a classical styled environment, where service and hospitality are very important. A four-star hotel with five-star service. An environment where international guests and locals alike feel welcome and at home.

What is the challenge in designing a hotel environment?
To be sure that there is a connection between the users, guests, and operational staff. That there can be discoveries to make, giving guests an experience that's real, not over-designed.

Are there any other hotels you find particularly inspiring?
The Setai Miami – a strong and straight balance in architecture and a powerful staff. There are a lot of hotels which are inspiring – for FG Stijl, mostly grand hotels and historic hotels.

How does the College Hotel differ from a hotel you would have built with your own money?
Not at all. We spend our client's money as carefully as if it were our own. In the end it has to be in balance, economically, commercially and socially.

What kind of travelers did you have in mind when you were designing this hotel?
International guests and locals. It must be a place where it all happens. A busy hotel and restaurant/bar is the best place to learn with demanding guests.

Neri Hotel & Restaurante
Barcelona, Spain

In Barcelona, home of some of the world's most astonishing modern architecture, there's one sure-fire way for a new hotel to swim against the current; in this town, the mere act of adapting an existing structure seems almost avant-garde. And rather than occupy some sparkling white tower or rakish postmodern monument, the Hotel Neri makes its home in a seventeenth-century palace, deep down the winding alleyways of the ancient Jewish Quarter.

Approaching the hotel through the pedestrian-only historic district, past the cathedral and the tiny square devoted to Saint Felip Neri, one is perhaps more prepared to find an old-fashioned bed and breakfast or a classic antique-style hotel – there's certainly no hint of anything modern among the neighborhood's quaint cafés and tourist traps. Behind its aged stone walls, however, the Neri is centuries removed from its Gothic surroundings.

The interiors are contemporary in style, but at once more sensuous and less pretentious than the typical design hotel. If the Nineties were a decade of explosive ostentatiousness, then the current one at its best is marked by a

measure of subtlety, and a preference for tactile pleasures above mere eye candy. Cheap thrills could have been had juxtaposing trendy, shiny interiors against the building's original stonework, but owner Bruno Figueras and designer Cristina Gabà have opted for a lighter touch, a restraint that plays well to the subdued charms of this urban hideaway.

There's little in the way of flash, then, but plenty of creativity, whether unusual lighting effects or slightly strange yet fully functional pieces of furniture. And there's plenty of unfussy new-school luxury as well, from the stylish fixtures set against the unpolished stone of the bathroom to the efficient gadgetry of the bedrooms, complete with flat-screen televisions and smart work desks. Natural light works its way in through balcony windows and the occasional bathroom porthole, but there's above all a hint of the distinctly Spanish predilection for slightly dim interiors, softening the edge of the lighter-toned rooms and intensifying the depth and richness of the darker, more masculine ones. There's a faint line between the clean and simple lines of a well-executed contemporary hotel interior and the sort of minimalism that's quickly starting to look dated – happily, these rooms land on the right side of that line every time.

Just as much stress is placed on the restaurant as on the rooms; the Neri's restaurant goes beyond the scope of the typical hotel kitchen, and is an authentic success among the locals, dealing in an unpretentious and confident Mediterranean cuisine, with an approach that's right in line with the hotel's philosophy of quietly understated luxury. Service here, as in the hotel, is outstanding, remaining crisply professional even at such a small and intimate scale.

Most surprising is the rooftop terrace and garden, quite literally a breath of fresh air, a contrast with the cloistered spaces of the hotel and the neighborhood. Here guests loll on lounge chairs and bask in the views of the cathedral and the Gothic Quarter, sipping coffee or cocktails or cooling off under an outdoor shower. By night, it's a candle-lit escape, an unexpectedly romantic hiding place, and a pleasant addition to an already inspiring environment.

SOLARIUM

Sezz
Paris, France

Whilst some Parisian hotel interiors edge ever closer to the realm of self-parody, many talented local artists strive to create something that's contemporary yet distinctly Parisian. One such designer is Christophe Pillet, a one-time Starck protégé who has set out on his own. With Sezz, his objective is to strike an original path between two antithetical trends: the century-old yet distinctly French hotel style of antique furnishings and fabric-covered walls, and the current yet faceless international style of minimalist hotels.

Sezz is the name of the hotel, a pun on its location in the 16th arrondissement, a quiet and largely residential district whose tree-lined streets and harmonious classic façades are the postcard image of traditional Paris. All the more intense, then, is the contrasting note struck by these highly idiosyncratic interiors.

The hotel is something of a shelter, rather than the gathering place so many boutiques aspire to be, a private refuge far from the avenues frequented by tourists and revelers. Obvious references to Zen gardens, though, are studiously

avoided. The look is something more timeless than modern, with dark greys and splashes of bright color instead of coat after coat of white. Rich textures of rough stone and lacquered wood are emphasized over simple optical thrills, resulting in a space that subtly attracts the eye, rather than dazzling it.

A sense of originality comes from subtle decisions like the layout of the bedrooms: the beds, most often, lie in the center of the room, with the desk behind, acting as a headboard. Thick shag carpets in deep reds or greens strike an almost retro note. Bathrooms sit behind glass walls, and there's an endless variety of bathtubs, some squarish and slightly Japanese in style, mounted into wooden consoles built into the walls.

Ironically, for all the studious avoidance of Zen clichés, there exists a touch of the minimal about the place, owing to a confident and pared-down design, free of visual gimmickry. The hotel's public spaces feel private, less like a catwalk and more like a lounge than the typical design hotel lobby. There's no groovy bar scene being cultivated here; even the Veuve Cliquot champagne bar feels more like a private club than a flashy hotel nightspot.

The look of the Sezz isn't quite the whole story. Service here operates on a unique concept: there's no reception and no bellhops or concierge, just an army of free-floating and multi-skilled "personal assistants," each competent to handle any guest request or tackle any unexpected issue. It's a bit like one imagines staying at a grand old country house would have been, with a personal valet on loan for the duration of your stay – a highly personalized experience, and one quite unlike that on offer in most modern hotels.

In the end, it's one of the most unique hotels we've seen; neither modern nor retro, neither international nor typically Parisian, the Sezz is a completely individual expression, and one that successfully challenges what we expect from a contemporary boutique hotel. Chances are you'll find yourself missing it when you're away, and planning trips to Paris just to see it again – and if that's not the measure of a successful hotel, then we don't know what is.

INTERVIEW WITH SHAHÉ KALAIDJIAN, OWNER OF SEZZ

What was your original vision for this hotel?
It's my version of what a 21st-century hotel should be like. A Haute-Couture hotel which would last for years. The concept was not to have a reception, not to have a segregation of specialties for employees, but to have employees who are capable of taking care of you from A to Z, rather than going to the concierge for a taxi, going to reception for check-in. This is what I believe service should be.

Was it a difficult birth process?
Yes. Of course. Every project is. And I think it was especially challenging because of the neighborhood we are in, and the administration we had to deal with. Every time we opened a new door somebody shut a new door in our faces. It was a bit of an anticlimax at the end. We worked so hard for years to make it happen, and when it opened, it was like "now what?"

How does the hotel differ from your vision?
It's not a question of the design. I think it's mainly what I wanted to achieve with regard to the technology. Some of the partners couldn't keep up, didn't have the products or the tools to develop what I wanted to develop. It's been a technological letdown, but it hasn't been a handicap. The client hasn't noticed.

With regard to the aesthetic side, probably there are one or two small details that you wouldn't even notice but in general I think Christophe achieved what I wanted to achieve. The idea of open spaces, keeping everything small, the fact that there are no barriers between the guest and the personnel, the concept of putting the bed in the center of the room.

Are you already thinking about the next hotel?
I'm not only thinking about the next hotel, but I'm also thinking of what I would like to do for example with Christophe next. My concept is, if I work with Christophe, I don't want to do a second hotel with Christophe in Paris. I think Paris should just have one Sezz, one Christophe and Shahé project. I think there are lots of possibilities. There are other cities to build in, I hope.

Have you learned any lessons that you think you could apply to the next one?
I think the most important thing is trying to work with good companies to finalize the work. We could be drawing things, I could tell Christophe I would like this like that, and if the guy who's doing it doesn't know how to do it, or he does it badly, we can draw as much as we want and it doesn't make a difference. I've learned also never to work with the best offer, the best value for money. In general a company I've worked with in the past, if they're good, I try to carry on working with them, even if they're not always the cheapest or most economical.

But each project is a new experience. I think that if I did another hotel tomorrow with Christophe in Cairo or in Dubai or London or New York, it would be a different experience again.

Can you describe the audience that this hotel has found?
There are people from all walks of life. What's interesting, more than the audience, is that a hotel like this has been snubbed by some industries. For example, we had a party here with fashion industry people, but they say "you're not in the Marais, so we can't come to you."

I think more people are choosing a hotel as a destination, not minding taking a taxi to go a little bit farther. From what I've noticed, people are choosing a destination as a function of what kind of establishment they want to be in, rather than the location. It's no longer "I want to be in the Marais so I'm going to go to the Novotel or the Holiday Inn or whatever." You look at what's pleasing to the eye before saying "I want to be in Bastille or St. Germain."

What do you find more exciting, creating the hotel, building it, or running it?
The first part, definitely. I'm a very bad manager. That's why I have good managers in place to do it. Definitely the creative side is the most exciting part. Trying to put in place the ideas, working the different materials, working with the designer, all this stuff for me is the most exciting.

Can you name hotels that inspire you?
Begawan Giri in Bali and Ksar Char Bagh in Marrakech.

INTERVIEW WITH CHRISTOPHE PILLET, DESIGNER OF SEZZ

How did you become involved in this project?
In a very natural and simple way. Shahé came to my place six or seven years ago just because he was interested in design, and we had a common friend. He wanted to see my work, he wanted to know me, and he explained to me that he was doing hotels. We became friends, and six or seven years after that he said "I have something for you."

What was the original brief?
There was no brief at all. Usually I don't work much with briefs. I had the costs, and some functionality. The brief we did together. Having discussions on what we think about hotels today, what this one should be, what it should not be. There was no client, no goals, no targets. It was an opportunity to spend some more time together, and it was enjoyable.

What would you say is the main challenge in designing a hotel?
The main challenge was to try to go one step beyond the nascent tradition of modern hotels. I didn't want to make a design hotel. The design hotel is something we've seen for about fifteen years, something invented by Ian Schrager and Philippe Starck a long time ago, and these hotels are really based on surprise, so they are more visual spaces than living spaces, making hotels more for the media than for the reality of spending time in the place.

We tried to start from the conceptual idea. Let's make something contemporary, but let's try not to be "design." From visual things to experimental living spaces. The quality you can see in the space is not based on the visual perception of things, but on the more intimate and personal impression. I think there is nothing impressive here. Everything is very normal. The attractiveness of this space comes from thousands of micro-details in balance. There is no big surprise, just mood.

The second step was saying, we are in Paris, let's make a Parisian hotel. It's now almost twenty years that we are living in this new international style, which has leveled tastes all over the planet.

I think it's important today to think local. Not in a reactionary way, but if I'm in New York, I really want to feel New York. If I go to Tokyo, I don't want to be in a New York style hotel, or a Bali style hotel, or an international abstract style hotel. I really believe the new modernity in design is more based on a reinterpretation of local culture than on universal things.

Everything, the choice of colors, the choice of materials, the mood, was really based on the fact that it is in Paris, and more than this, that it is in this area of Paris. I'm sure that if we had done a hotel in Bastille, it would have looked very different.

Can you name hotels that inspire you?
I love the Roppongi Hills hotel. But I don't have a hotel that inspires me completely. I can love some details and hate the hotel, or I can love a part of a hotel and dislike another part of it. I love the perfume of Blakes, in London. The smell is really a strong part of the emotion.

Would you rather design a church or a stadium?
Definitely not a church. Now the best buildings in the world are shopping centers and hotels.

Urban Hotel
Madrid, Spain

Madrid may be the more conservative of Spain's big cities, but there's plenty of modern design, made all the more striking by the contrast with the city's prevailing classic architecture, much of it dating to the 18th century and earlier. In the center of Habsburg Madrid, near the Puerta del Sol, stands the Hotel Urban, a stunning modern structure surrounded by centuries-old buildings, its metal and glass construction standing out against the neighboring stonework. Contemporary design isn't the whole story, though. The Urban may have the slightly edgy, industrial feel of the most stylish new boutiques, but it adds to this formula a generous helping of individuality.

Owner Jordi Clos is not just a successful hotelier but a noted art collector as well, and the head of an archaeological society whose collection the Urban was designed to display. A basement gallery houses a permanent collection of ancient Egyptian artworks, and the guest rooms are furnished with antique Hindu and Chinese pieces, complete with explanatory notes in the manner of a museum program. The result is engaging: while many high design hotels

resemble nothing so much as art galleries, with their blank white walls and minimalistic furnishings, the art is conspicuously absent. The Urban, in contrast, is a rich and warm, welcoming space, and the art-museum trappings don't even begin to introduce a note of sterility or emptiness.

The interior design in the public spaces is highly individual as well, with a particular emphasis on unusual lighting effects: a glowing alabaster column that descends the height of the atrium to the lobby floor, like a stream of molten rock being poured, and a reception desk made of the same luminescent material. Elsewhere six-foot fluorescent tubes line the walls, and globes dangle behind bar countertops, lit from within, again replicating the effect of white-hot stone or metal.

Upstairs, there's more to the guest rooms than ancient Hindu sculptures. Dark mahogany floors and black leather furnishings set a serious tone, and the amenities are up-to-the-minute, including flat-screen televisions and wireless internet access. Street-side windows are double-glazed to muffle the sounds of traffic, and the courtyard-side rooms are as quiet as Egyptian tombs.

Today's high-design hotels feature bathrooms that are as clever as the bedrooms, if not more so. These are behind glass walls, with fixtures as futuristic as any we've seen, from the conic wash basins to the deep stand-alone tubs. Heavy towels and robes are de rigueur for a hotel of the Urban's stature, as are custom-packaged bath products.

Located between the Puerta del Sol and the museum district, the Urban isn't short for competition in the restaurant and nightspot stakes; that it's such a success is remarkable indeed. The Europa Decó and the Glass Bar are among Madrid's hottest spots, but the real gem is the rooftop terrace. By day it's a pool deck, where guests lounge in the sun with a view of the city, and by night it's an open-air bar, with cocktail tables perched at the building's edge, six stories above the street.

GLASS
BAR

The Soho Hotel
London, England

In living memory Soho has changed from a neighborhood of decidedly ill repute to something rather more respectable; still one of London's most exciting places, it's simply moved a bit upmarket. The forces of gentrification have done their work, to be sure, and new loft spaces are still appearing, but the slightly seedy romance of Soho's past still hangs in the air.

More prosaically, this is the geographic heart of the British independent film industry and is, along with the nearby Strand, the center of the theater district, a fact that can't help but contribute to Soho's street life, in evidence long after the adjoining neighborhoods have been deserted for the night. Restaurants abound, in any number of styles, and the theater crowd mixes with the local literary types in the district's famous pubs and private clubs.

Around here you won't find a delicate Georgian townhouse hotel, or an imposing floodlit facade like those of the flashier grand hotels. Still largely unknown even to London's taxi drivers, the Soho Hotel sits back from Dean Street at the end of Richmond Mews, itself seemingly an unassuming back alley but for the grey-suited doorman and the occasional black cab making its turn beneath a constellation of tiny blue lights.

Upon entering, one is immediately confronted with the fact that this is anything but the ordinary city luxury hotel; the sedate wood-paneled reception, classic as can be, is menaced by a ten-foot statue of a black cat, hunched as though on the lookout for a giant mouse. This space is perfect as a first taste of Kit Kemp's style of interior decorating, a style which, though daring and modern, is fastidious in its avoidance of the minimalist and the futuristic. Instead it relies on traditional elements livened by unexpected contrasts – a sitting-room library, for example, whose shelves glow with a blue light from between rows of antique books, or a basement cinema with garish lipstick-red or cowhide-print leather armchairs.

Public spaces are easy enough for any hotelier with a bit of nerve – more tellingly, the Soho's guest rooms are exquisite as well, full of surprises like the full-sized dresser's dummy keeping watch over the sitting area, echoed in miniature by a smaller glass mannequin lamp glowing atop the desk. In some designers' hands, the lush fabrics and feminine colors of the wall coverings and upholstery could verge on preciousness. Here the soft touch is hardened by contrast with industrial-issue floor-to-ceiling windows and robust, outsize furnishings, resulting in an environment that's engagingly contemporary, in contrast with the transplanted country-house hotel aesthetic that's so widespread even in the heart of London.

There's more to these rooms than visual effect, of course. This place is about

luxury – not old-fashioned, antique-furniture delicacy, but a contemporary sort that's functional and friendly to the touch. Sprawling bathrooms feature spacious walk-in showers and deep tubs, outfitted with Miller Harris products and heated towel racks. And the hotel's facilities are impressive too, with a fitness center and spa downstairs, in addition to the meeting facilities and two exceptional private screening rooms. Refuel, the restaurant and bar, stays busy most nights of the week, with in-the-know locals wandering down Richmond Mews to mix with hotel guests against the backdrop of a mural depicting the Soho's illustrious former life as a multi-level car park. Like the rest of the hotel, it's equal parts high elegance and playful whimsy, and it feels exclusive in the manner of a guarded secret.

Perhaps it's that intangible feeling that's key to this hotel's appeal. The Soho isn't exclusive in the old snobbish and sniffy meaning of the word, but it does convey a certain sense of membership to those in the know, those patrons who like their luxury experience delivered with a wink and a bit of cleverness.

La Sommità Relais
Ostuni, Italy

The idea of Italy as a holiday destination brings with it certain expectations, certain familiar scenes – from the palazzos and canals of Venice to the streets of Rome, buzzing with motorbikes; from the red roofs and vineyard rows of Tuscany to the cliffside mansions of the Amalfi coast.

Ostuni, then, seems like another world. A knotty assemblage of white stone buildings, clustered together atop a hill that rises alone from the arid plains of Puglia's Adriatic coast, it's got a bit of the desert about it – the view from La Sommita's patio, over the whitewashed rooftops and clotheslines of the town, across miles of low olive trees to the edge of the sea, looks more like North Africa than it does the archetypal Italian landscape.

What seems like an unconventional choice for a location in fact plays directly to the hotel's strength. There's no sense that you're here to "do" Ostuni; though there's a charming Gothic cathedral, an endless supply of historic buildings and any number of picturesque alleyways to wander down, this is not the sort of place where you drop your luggage and rush into the town, snapping photos.

This is a retreat, a shelter, a moment of quiet in an overstimulated life, an environment that's meant to envelop rather than impress.

And though fashioned from a centuries-old palazzo, La Sommita isn't much to look at from the outside: in fact it's near impossible to tell where it ends and the adjoining buildings begin. The main entrance, at the end of a winding alleyway, feels as though it must be the side door, and the reception is discreetly tucked away half behind a staircase. Up the stairs, the nine (just nine!) suites, spread throughout the building in a calculatedly disorienting effect – the square geometry of the traditional hotel with its rows and columns of rooms is lost completely. Any sense of orientation with respect to the outside world is likely to be illusory: top-floor bathrooms feel like basement vaults, and every suite feels as though it could be the only suite.

The interiors walk the line between an ascetic minimalism and a stylish luxury, in a palette of creams and off-whites, with the sort of quiet and solid furnishings that are the signifiers of high-end modern interior design. The Culti name is in evidence, but discreetly so: though practically a showroom for the Italian lifestyle brand, the trademark is apparent only on the bottles containing the bath amenities and on the necks of the alarmingly solid clothes hangers.

The vast bathroom may yet be the centerpiece of each suite: with walls of stone blocks, and curved ceilings coming to a point at a small skylight, they evoke an atmosphere like that of a hidden underground spa. A massive tub sits at one end, framed by an archway, and alongside it a substantial heap of towels and robes, along with a generous assortment of the house brand's bath products.

Downstairs, an old olive press has made way for an intimate restaurant, with a handful of tables under an arched stone ceiling, and spilling out onto the shaded and quiet patio terrace. Here a decidedly modern Italian cuisine is on offer, an austere simplicity relying on top-quality local ingredients. Service is modern as well, relaxed and unpretentious in a way that well serves the atmosphere of this small hotel.

There's a private beach a short shuttle ride away, and a selection of massage and spa treatments on offer in the vault below the restaurant, and if you're up for a bit of exploring, Ostuni's old town is packed with cafes and restaurants. The hotel, though, inspires meditation above all else. It's the opposite of the dazzling pyrotechnic effects of Italy's grand old palace hotels; with no sea view, Renaissance architecture or uniformed bellmen making a show of old-fashioned hospitality, La Sommita is a perfectly hypnotic escape, a sedate and sequestered place to disappear for a day or a week. It hardly feels like a traditional hotel at all, and is all the more restful and relaxing for it.

CULTI
FRAGRANZA NATURALE
PER AMBIENTE

Index

Hotel Fox
Jarmers Plads 3
DK-1551 Copenhagen V, Denmark
Tel: +45.33.13.30.00
Fax: +45.33.14.30.33

61 rooms and suites
Published rates starting at DKK 945
for a "small" room
All rates are per room per night
and include breakfast, service and 25% V.A.T.

Style: Cutting-Edge
Atmosphere: Lively
Owners: Broechner family
Lead Architect/Designer: Anders Saelan

The Zetter Restaurant & Rooms
St John's Square
86-88 Clerkenwell Road
London EC1M 5RJ, UK
Tel: +44.(0)20.7324.4444
Fax: +44.(0)20.7324.4445

59 rooms and suites
Published rates starting at £135
for a "guest" room
All rates are excluding 17.5% V.A.T.

Style: Modern Design
Atmosphere: Happening
Owner: Mark Sainsbury
Lead Architect/Designer: Laurie Chetwood

The College Hotel
Roelof Hartstraat 1
1071 VE Amsterdam, Netherlands
Tel: +31.(0)20.57.11.511
Fax: +31.(0)20.57.11.512

40 rooms and suites
Published rates starting at € 175
for a "superior single" room
All rates are excluding 5% city tax

Style: Contemporary Classic
Atmosphere: Lively
Owner: ROC van Amsterdam
Lead Architect/Designer: FG-Stijl

Urban Hotel
Carrera de San Jerónimo, 34
Madrid 28014, Spain
Tel: +34.91.787.7770
Fax: +34.91.787.7799

96 rooms and suites
Published rates starting at € 175
for an "individual" room
All rates are excluding 7% tax

Style: Cutting-Edge
Atmosphere: Happening
Owner: Jordi Clos Llombart
Lead Architect/Designer: Carles Bassó
and Mariano Martitegui

Neri Hotel & Restaurante
C/ Sant Sever, 5
Barcelona 08002, Spain
Tel: +34 93.304.0655
Fax: +34 93.304.0337

22 rooms and suites
Published rates starting at € 215
for a "standard double" room
All rates are excluding 7% tax

Style: Modern Design
Atmosphere: Lively
Owner: Bruno Figueras
Lead Architect/Designer: Cristina Gabas

L'Andana
c/o Tenuta La Badiola, Località Badiola,
Castiglione della Pescaia
Grosseto 58043, Italy
Tel: +39.0564.944.800
Fax: +39.0564.944.577

33 rooms and suites
Published rates starting at € 440
for a "deluxe double" room
All rates are including tax and service charges

Style: Traditional Elegance
Atmosphere: Secluded
Owners: Vittorio Moretti and Alain Ducasse
Lead Architect/Designer: Ettore Mocchetti

Sezz
6 avenue Frémiet
75016 Paris, France
Tel: +33.(0)1.56.75.26.26
Fax:+33.(0)1.56.75.26.16

27 rooms and suites
Published rates starting at € 225
for a "single" room
All rates are including tax and service charges

Style: Cutting-Edge
Atmosphere: Quiet
Owner: Shahé Kalaidjian
Lead Architect/Designer: Christophe Pillet

The Bvlgari Hotel
Via Privata Fratelli Gabba 7/b
20121 Milano, Italy
Tel: +39.02.805.805.1
Fax: +39.02.805.805.222

52 rooms and suites
Published rates starting at € 650
for a "deluxe" room
All rates are excluding 10% tax

Style: Modern Design
Atmosphere: Quiet
Owner: Bvlgari
Lead Architect/Designer: Antonio Citterio

La Sommità Relais
Via Scipione Petrarolo 7
Ostuni ,Italy
Tel: +39.0831.305925
Fax: +39.0831.306729

9 suites
Published rates starting at € 250
for a "double" room
All rates are including tax and service charges

Style: Contemporary Classic
Atmosphere: Quiet
Owner: Culti

The Soho Hotel
4 Richmond Mews
London W1D 3DH, UK
Tel: +44 20 7559 3000
Fax: +44 20 7559 3003

91 rooms and suites
Published rates starting at £235
for a "superior double" room
All rates are excluding 17.5% V.A.T.

Style: Modern Design
Atmosphere: Happening
Owners: Tim & Kit Kemp
Interior Designer: Kit Kemp

Go to **TabletHotels.com**
for real-time availability
information and special rates.

A **Tablet Hotels** Book

First published in December 2005 by Tablet Inc.
37 West 17th Street, New York, NY 10011, USA

Tablet Hotels is a registered trademark of Tablet Inc.

Web site at: **www.TabletHotels.com**

Library of Congress Cataloging-in-Publication Data upon request

Library of Congress Control Number: 2005909702

ISBN 0-9774971-0-0

Photography by Jorge Bustos for all properties except Sezz
Photography of Sezz by Manuel Zublena
Texts by John Speranza
Edited by Laurent Vernhes
Page design by Juliette Cezzar

Printed and bound in the USA